KUSUDAMA
BALL ORIGAMI

Makoto Yamaguchi

D1534393

Shufunotomo/Japan Publications

Tokyo, Japan

If you would like more information about Origami in
America, please send a self-addressed envelope
with 2 first class stamps to:

The Friends of the Origami Center of America
Box JP-1
15 West 77th Street
New York, NY 10024-5192

10 9 8 7 6

© Copyright in Japan 1990 by Makoto Yamaguchi

Published by Shufunotomo Co., Ltd.
2-9, Kanda Surugadai, Chiyoda-ku, Tokyo, 101 Japan

Distributors:
UNITED STATES: Kodansha International USA/Ltd, through Farrar,
Straus & Giroux, 19 Union Square West, New York, NY 10003.
CANADA: Fitzhenry & Whiteside Ltd., 195 Allstate Parkway,
Markham, Ontario L3R 4T8. BRITISH ISLES AND EUROPEAN
CONTINENT: Premier Book Marketing Ltd., 1 Gower Street, London
WC1E 6HA. AUSTRALIA AND NEW ZEALAND: Bookwise
International, 54 Crittenden Road, Findon, South Australia 5023.
THE FAR EAST AND JAPAN: Japan Publications Trading Co., Ltd.,
1-2-1, Sarugaku-cho, Chiyoda-ku, Tokyo 101.

ISBN 0-87040-863-1

Printed in Japan

KUSUDAMA is a decorative paper ball for festive occasions. Originally it was an ornamental scent bag hung to clear away noxious vapors, thus the name "*KUSU*" (medicine) + "*DAMA*" (ball). Origami works are usually made from one piece of square paper, but *Kusudama Origami* is different. It combines several units of origami. Folding each piece and then joining the units with the completed ball in mind is an enjoyable process. No intricate methods are involved; folding and joining the units is simple and easy.

This is a basic book for beginners. The step-by-step illustrations are clear, and there is no guesswork. A completed *Kusudama* makes a wonderful present, and is indispensable as a Christmas decoration.

SYMBOLS FOR FOLDING

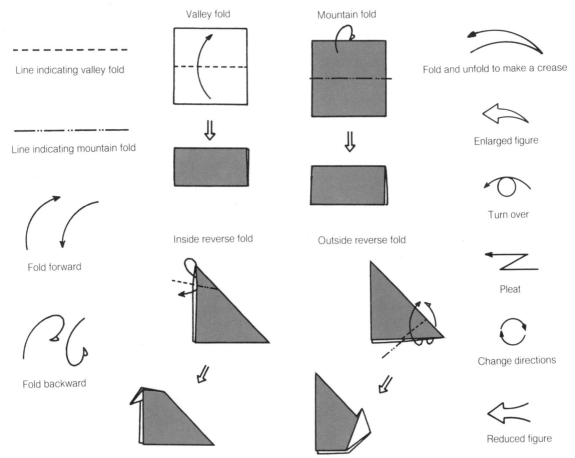

Line indicating valley fold

Line indicating mountain fold

Fold forward

Fold backward

Valley fold

Mountain fold

Inside reverse fold

Outside reverse fold

Fold and unfold to make a crease

Enlarged figure

Turn over

Pleat

Change directions

Reduced figure

CONTENTS

PLUTO
(See page 50.)

BLEEZE
(See page 34.)

DICE
(See page 42.)

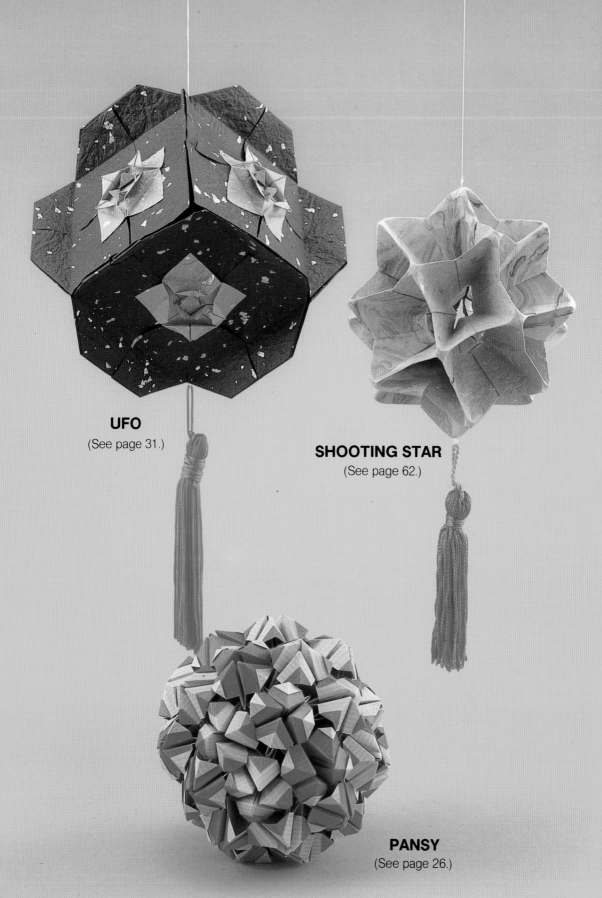

UFO
(See page 31.)

SHOOTING STAR
(See page 62.)

PANSY
(See page 26.)

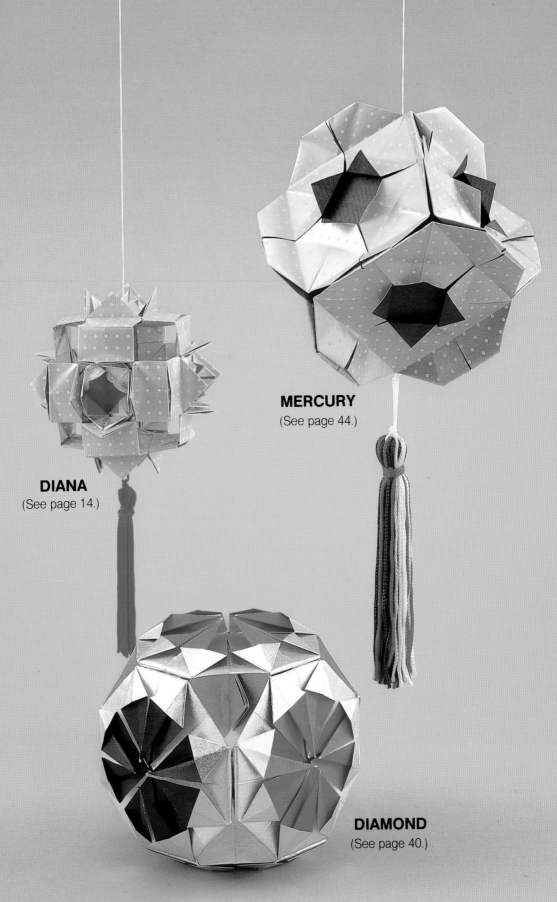

MERCURY
(See page 44.)

DIANA
(See page 14.)

DIAMOND
(See page 40.)

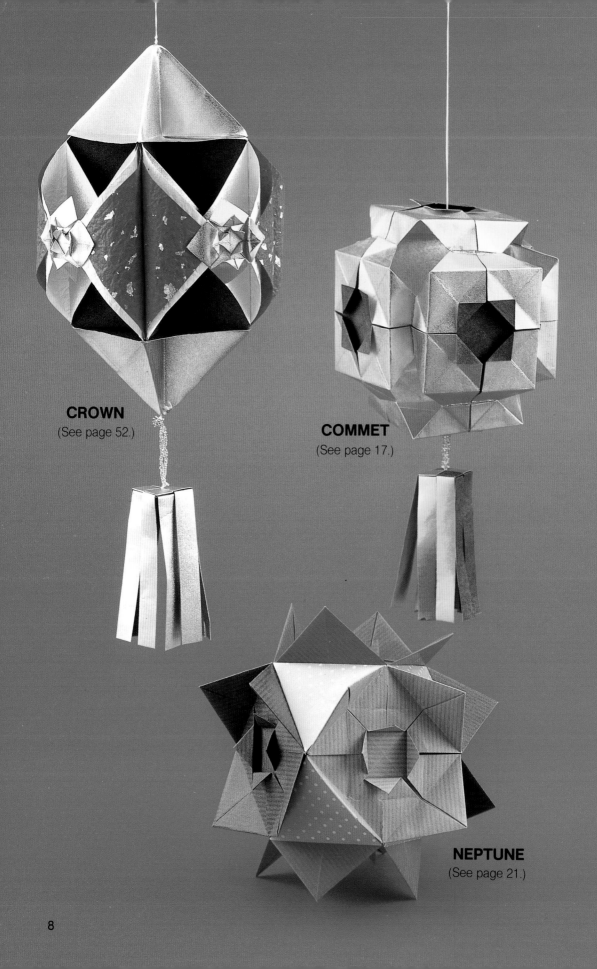

CROWN
(See page 52.)

COMMET
(See page 17.)

NEPTUNE
(See page 21.)

8

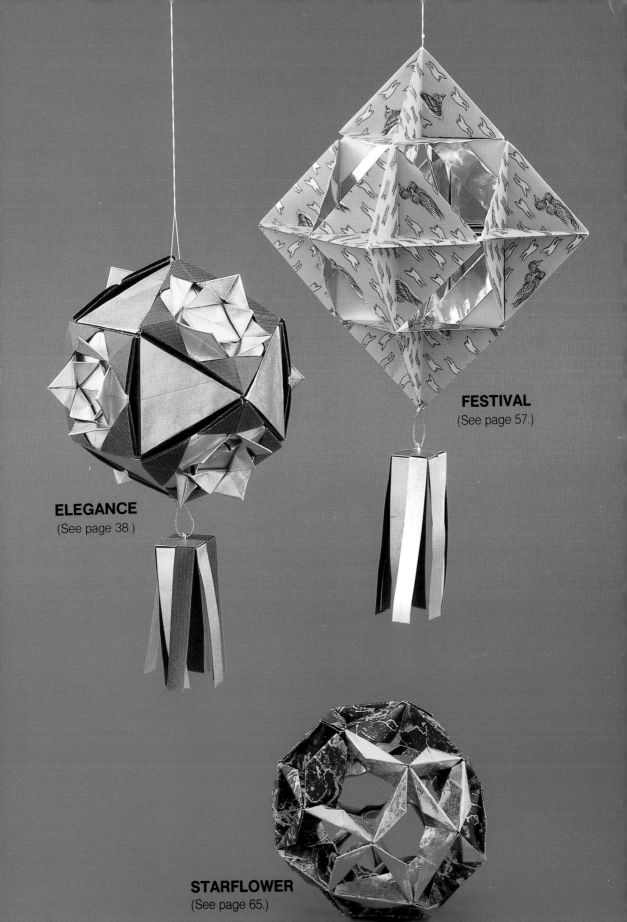

ELEGANCE
(See page 38.)

FESTIVAL
(See page 57.)

STARFLOWER
(See page 65.)

9

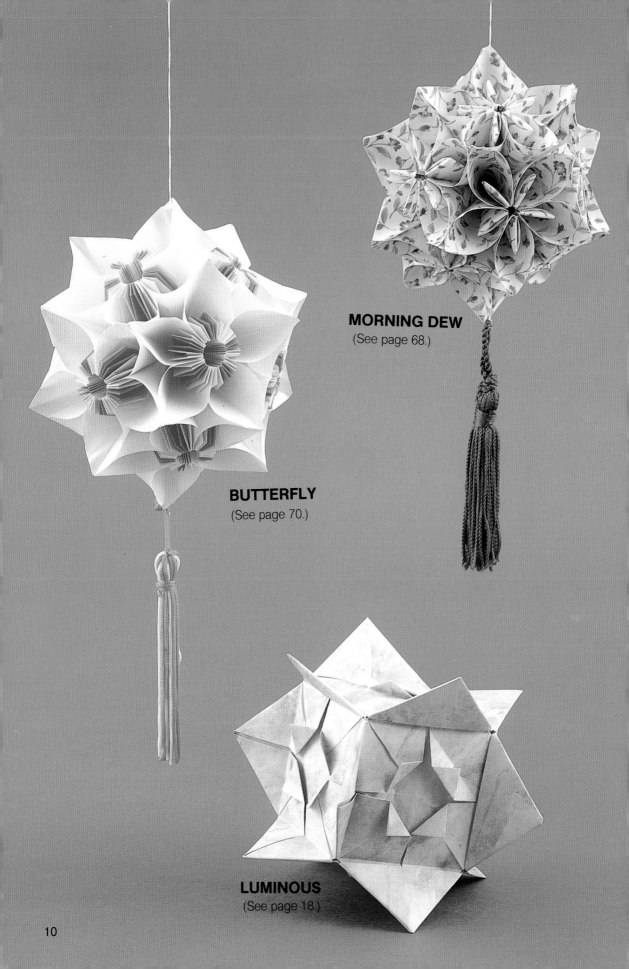

MORNING DEW
(See page 68.)

BUTTERFLY
(See page 70.)

LUMINOUS
(See page 18.)

10

VENUS
(See page 46.)

1

Open the string with the bunch of yarn and put a group of assembled units on it.

2

First, insert the marked string into any slit of the units and then the other string in the following order: the second string into the second slit from the first string, the third string into the third slit from the second string, and the fourth string into the second slit from the third string.

3

Put the second group of units on top of the first group, and thread the marked string through the second group, and the other strings in the following order: the second string into the third slit, the third string into the second slit, and the fourth string into the third slit.

4

FIRST & THIRD GROUPS	SECOND & FOURTH GROUPS

FIRST & THIRD GROUPS

2 units
3 units   3 units
2 units

SECOND & FOURTH GROUPS

3 units
2 units   2 units
3 units

Put the third and fourth groups and thread the strings as illustrated.

5

Pull the strings one by one and shape the whole carefully.

7

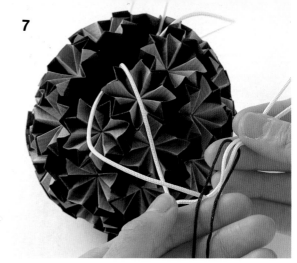

Thread the string through the loop of the hanger.

6

Hold each of two strings together and make a loose knot in the center and pull the string slowly. When the knot comes to the base, fasten it tightly so that the whole makes a round ball.

8

Tie twice firmly as in step 6.

9

Cut the strings near the base. Completed.

KUSUDAMA
BALL ORIGAMI

DIANA

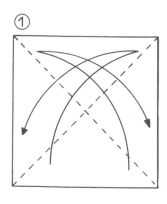

Make creases.

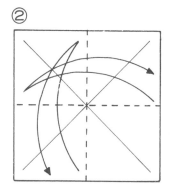

Make creases.

BLINTZ FOLD

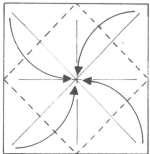

Fold the four corners to the center.

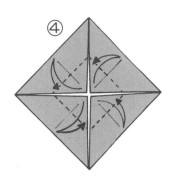

Make creases.

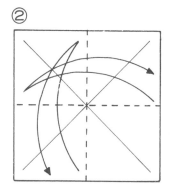

Fold the point to the crease.

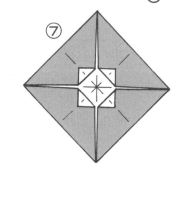

Fold the other points in the same way.

14

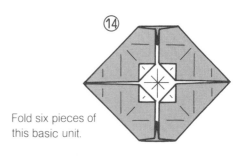

Fold six pieces of
this basic unit.

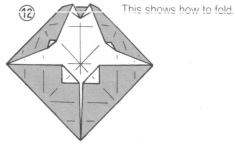

Fold the opposite corner in
the same way.

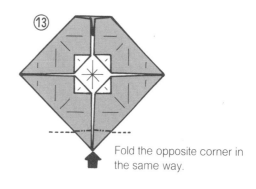

This shows how to fold.

Fold so that the marked
part comes inside.

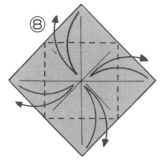

Make creases.

Open the upper layers.

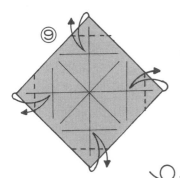

Make creases.

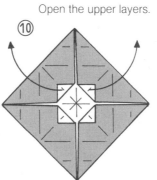

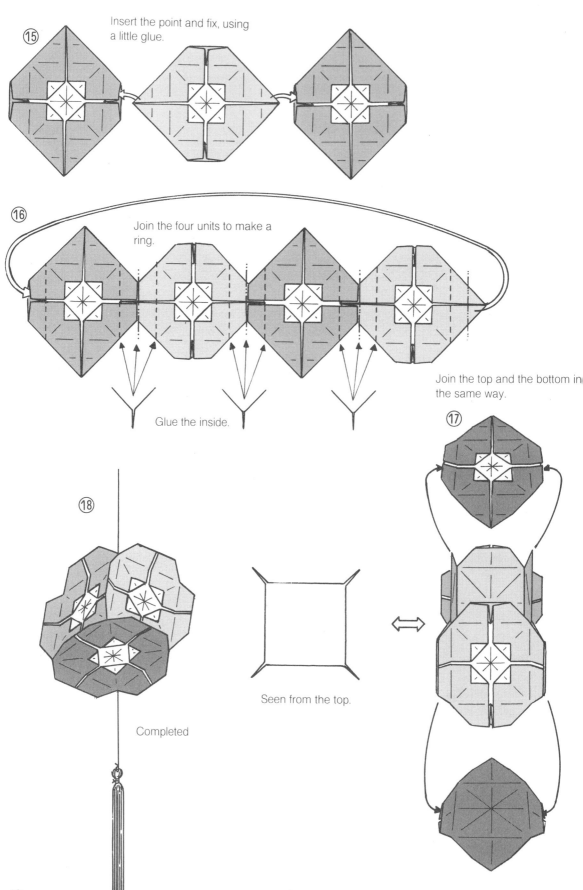

⑮ Insert the point and fix, using a little glue.

⑯ Join the four units to make a ring.

Glue the inside.

Join the top and the bottom in the same way.

⑰

⑱

Seen from the top.

Completed

16

COMMET

Combine four units and join them.

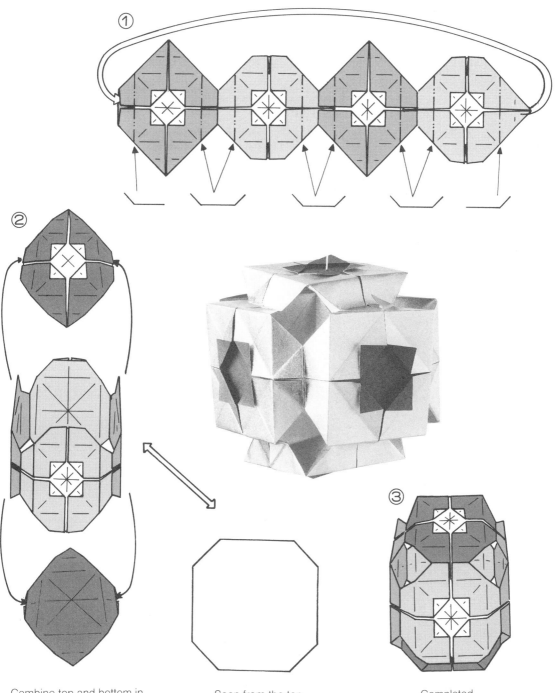

①

②

③

Combine top and bottom in
the same way.

Seen from the top.

Completed.

LUMINOUS

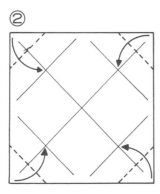

Fold the four corners up to the creases.

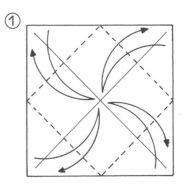

Make creases.

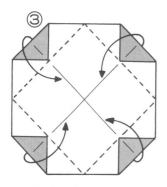

Fold on the creases.

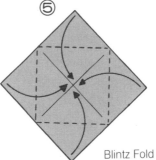

Fold the points as shown.

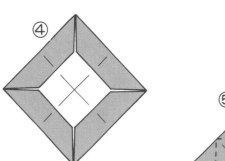

Blintz Fold

⑫

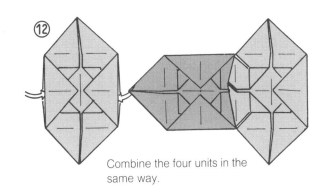

Combine the four units in the same way.

⑪

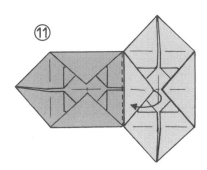

Lift one corner of the triangle.

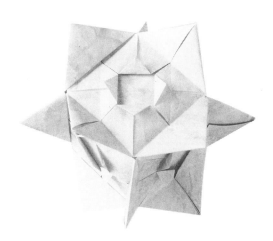

⑩

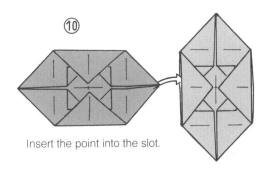

Insert the point into the slot.

⑦

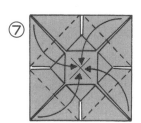

Blintz Fold

⑧

Open the two flaps.

⑨

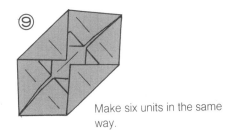

Make six units in the same way.

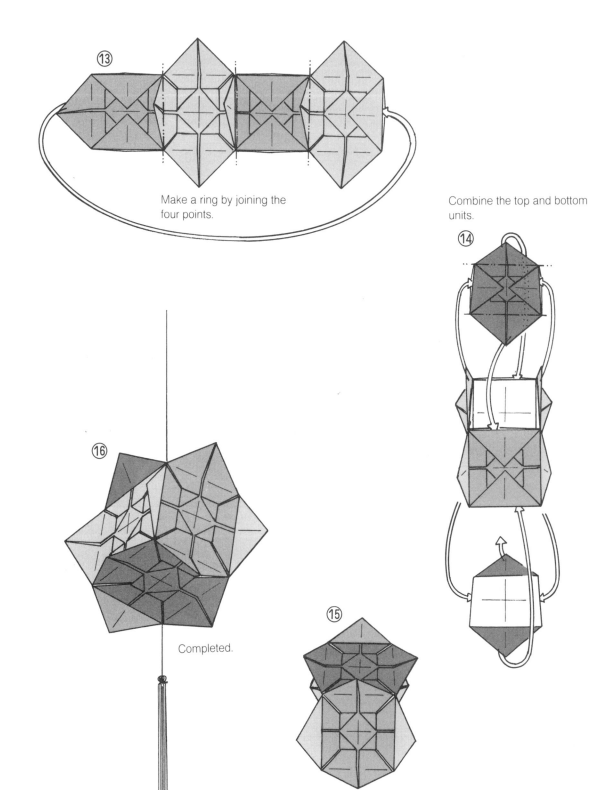

⑬

Make a ring by joining the four points.

Combine the top and bottom units.

⑭

⑯

Completed.

⑮

NEPTUNE

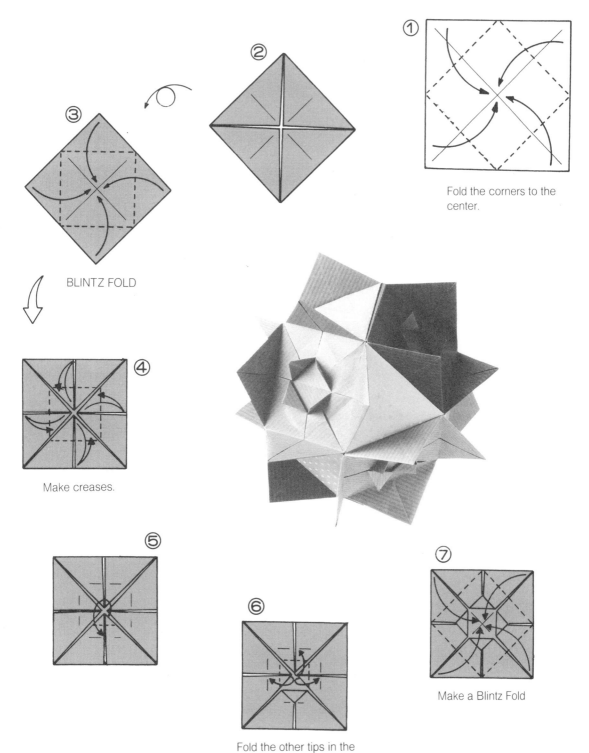

① Fold the corners to the center.

②

③ BLINTZ FOLD

④ Make creases.

⑤

⑥ Fold the other tips in the same way.

⑦ Make a Blintz Fold

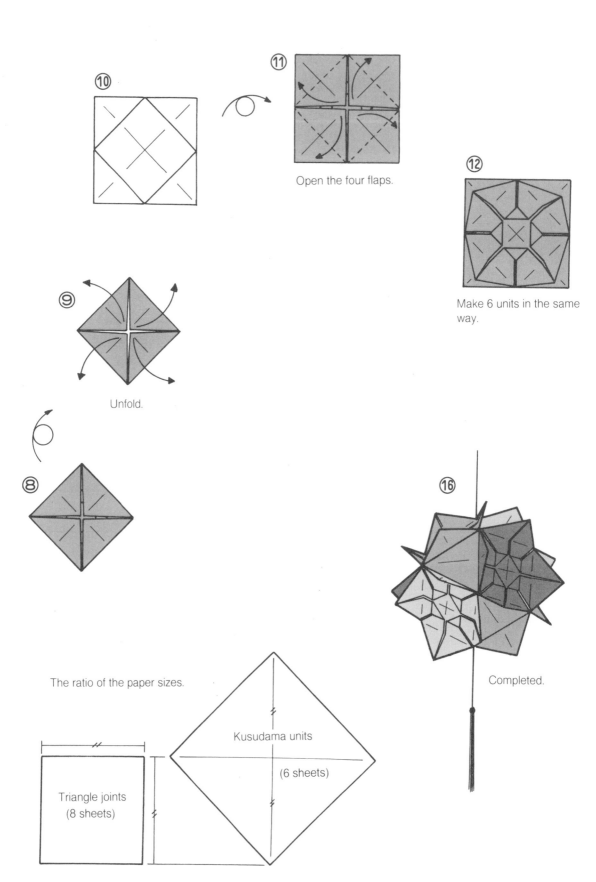

⑩

⑪

Open the four flaps.

⑫

Make 6 units in the same way.

⑨

Unfold.

⑧

The ratio of the paper sizes.

Kusudama units

(6 sheets)

Triangle joints
(8 sheets)

⑯

Completed.

22

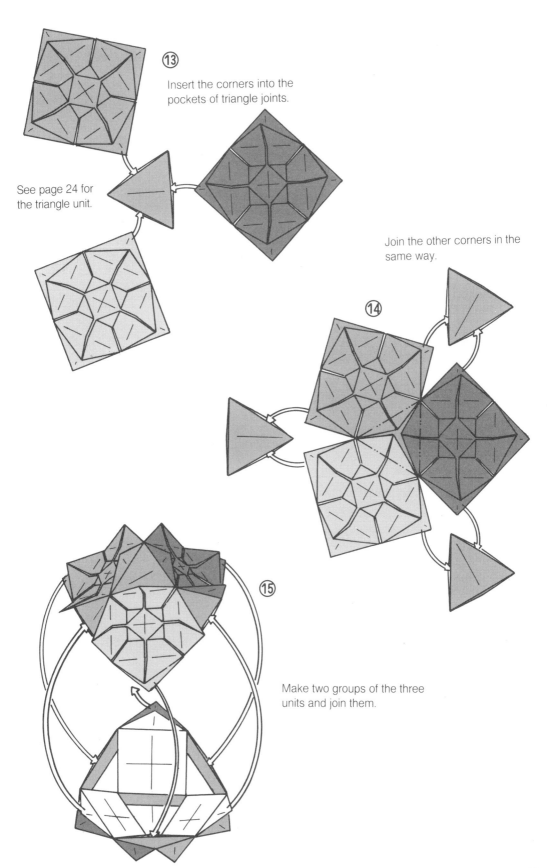

⑬ Insert the corners into the pockets of triangle joints.

See page 24 for the triangle unit.

Join the other corners in the same way.

⑭

⑮

Make two groups of the three units and join them.

TRIANGLE UNIT

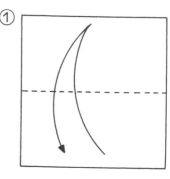

① Make a crease.

② Bring (B) to the center crease.

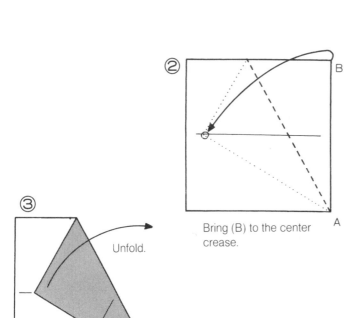

③ Unfold.

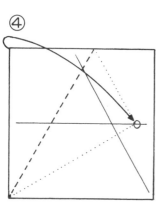

④ Repeat the same fold as in step 2.

Slots

⑤ Unfold.

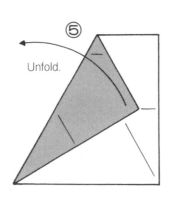

⑥ Fold over at the intersecting point.

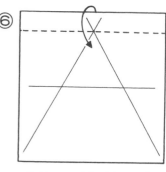

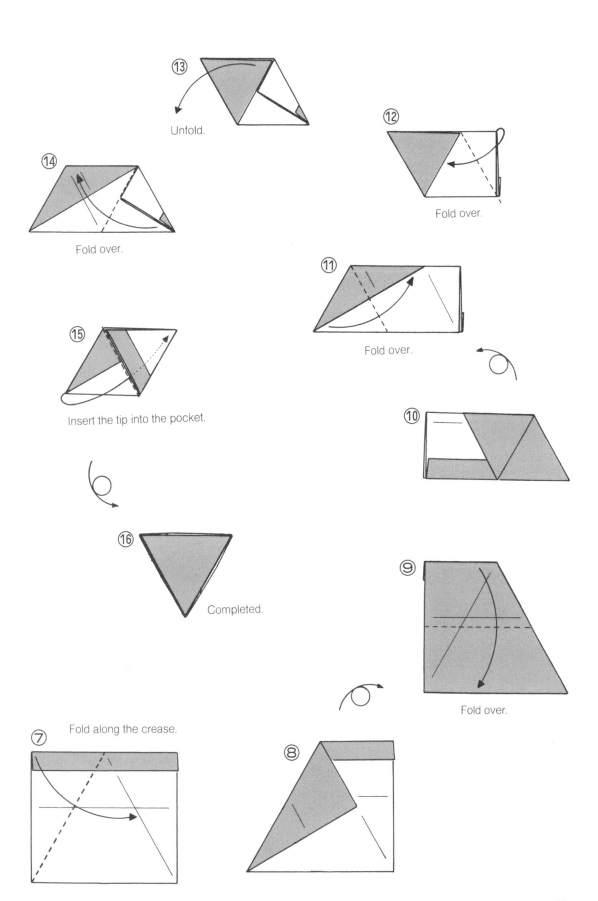

⑬ Unfold.

⑫ Fold over.

⑭ Fold over.

⑪ Fold over.

⑮ Insert the tip into the pocket.

⑩

⑯ Completed.

⑨ Fold over.

Fold along the crease.

⑦

⑧

TASSEL

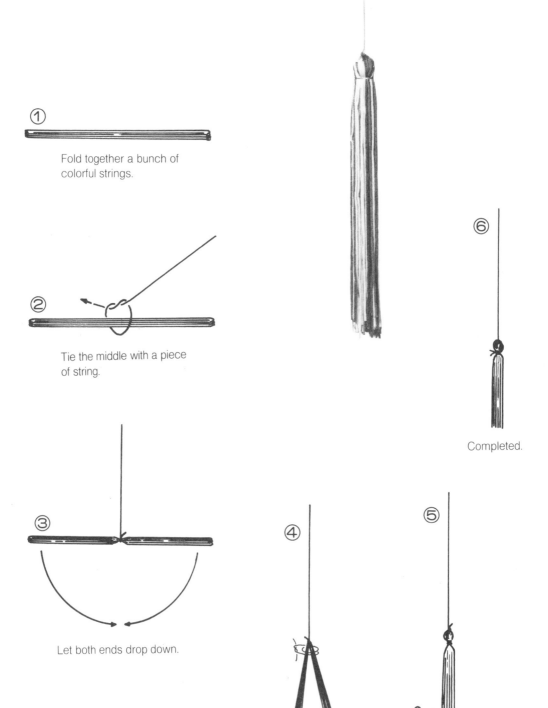

① Fold together a bunch of colorful strings.

② Tie the middle with a piece of string.

③ Let both ends drop down.

④ Tie the base of the bunch.

⑤ Trim the end.

⑥ Completed.

PAPER TASSEL

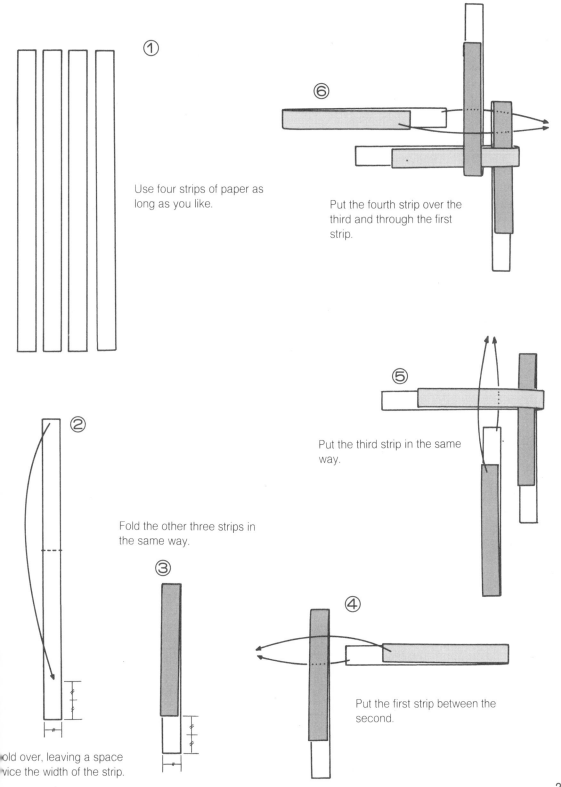

① Use four strips of paper as long as you like.

⑥ Put the fourth strip over the third and through the first strip.

⑤ Put the third strip in the same way.

② Fold the other three strips in the same way.

Fold over, leaving a space twice the width of the strip.

③

④ Put the first strip between the second.

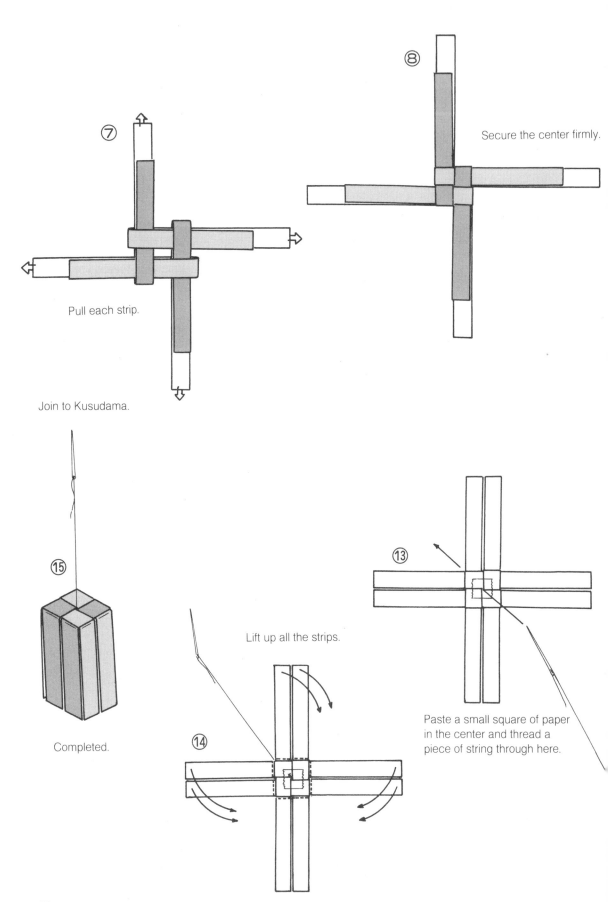

⑦ Pull each strip.

⑧ Secure the center firmly.

Join to Kusudama.

⑮ Completed.

Lift up all the strips.

⑭

⑬ Paste a small square of paper in the center and thread a piece of string through here.

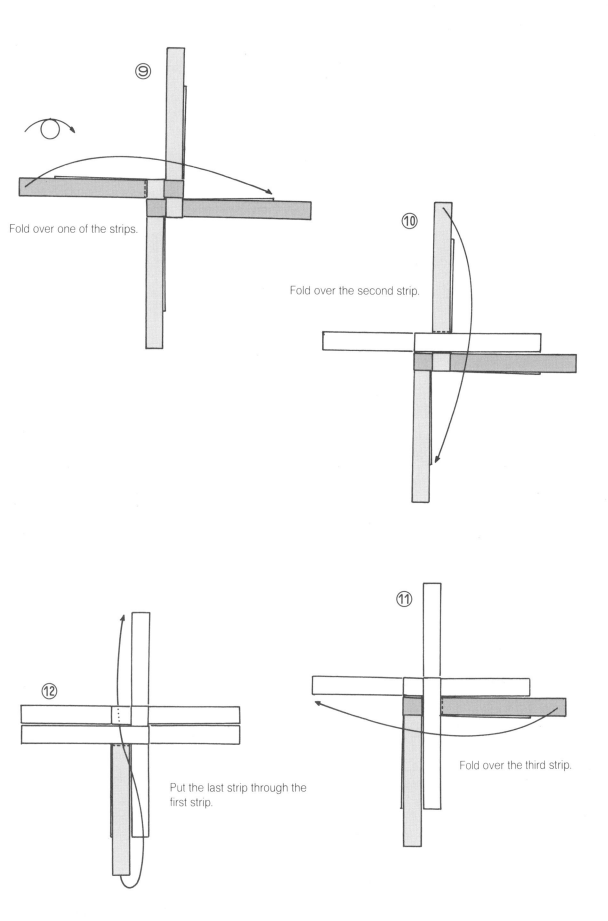

⑨

Fold over one of the strips.

⑩

Fold over the second strip.

⑪

Fold over the third strip.

⑫

Put the last strip through the first strip.

29

FLOWER PART

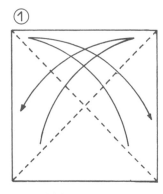

① Make creases.

BLINTZ FOLD

② Bring the four corners to the center.

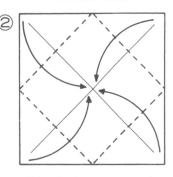

③

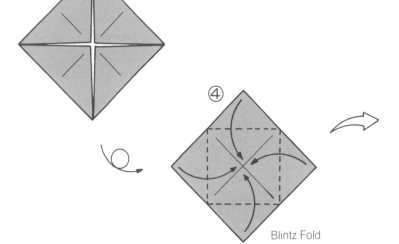

④ Blintz Fold

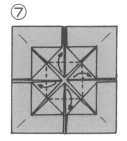

⑤ Fold so that the underside triangles come out.

⑥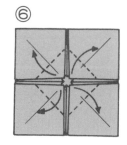

Fold and open the upper layers.

⑦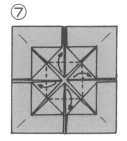

Also fold the underneath triangles.

⑧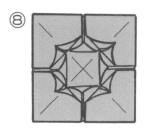

Completed.

UFO

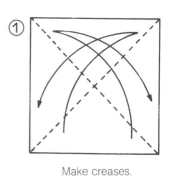

① Make creases.

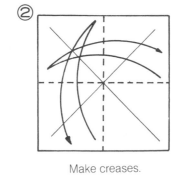

② Make creases.

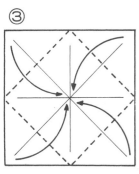

③ Blintz Fold.

④

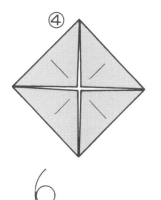

⑤ Make creases.

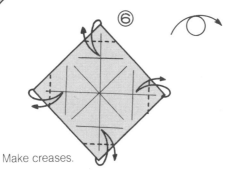

⑥ Make creases.

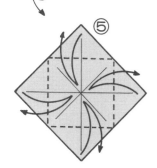

⑦ Push inward the marked parts.

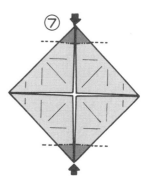

⑧ Unfold.

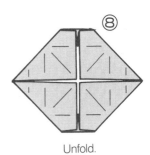

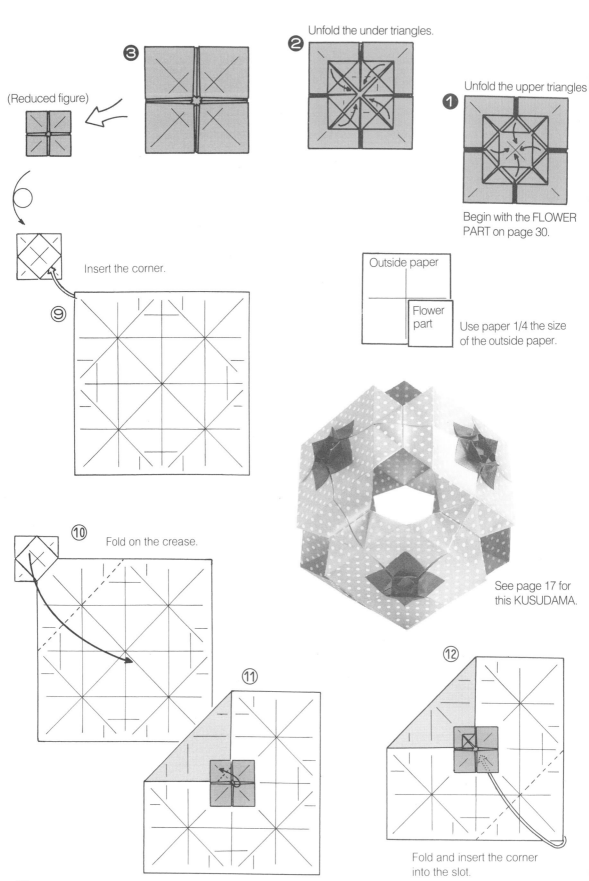

③ (Reduced figure)

② Unfold the under triangles.

① Unfold the upper triangles

Begin with the FLOWER PART on page 30.

Insert the corner.

⑨

Outside paper

Flower part

Use paper 1/4 the size of the outside paper.

See page 17 for this KUSUDAMA.

⑩ Fold on the crease.

⑪

⑫

Fold and insert the corner into the slot.

Fold and open the upper corner.

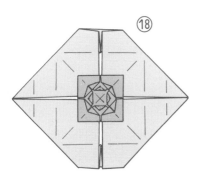

(18)

Make 6 of this unit, and assemble
the units in the same way as
shown on pages 16 and 17.

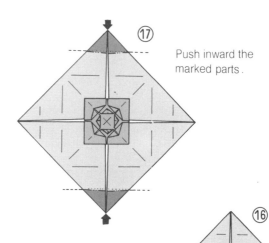

(17)

Push inward the
marked parts.

Completed.

See page 16 for this KUSUDAMA.

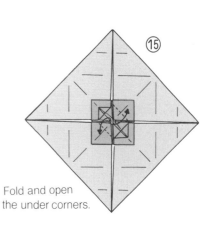

(16)

Fold and open
the under triangles.

(15)

Fold and open
the under corners.

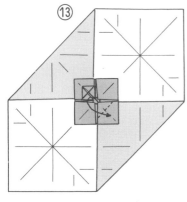

(13)

Fold and open the upper
corner.

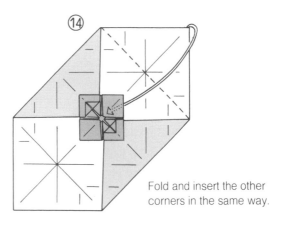

(14)

Fold and insert the other
corners in the same way.

33

BLEEZE

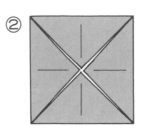

②

③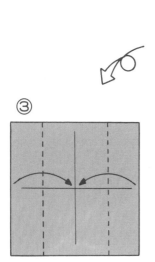

Fold over to the center line.

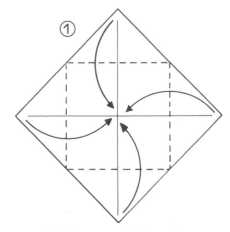

Fold the corners to the center.

④

⑨

Repeat the same fold on the other side.

⑧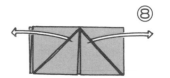

Pull out the corners.

⑤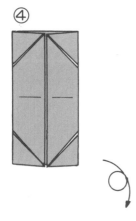

⑥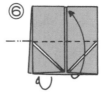

⑦

Fold the corners in triangles.

Fold in half.

Fold both sides in the same way.

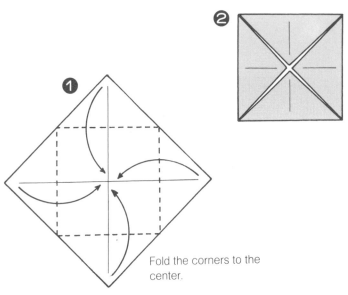

❷

❶

Fold the corners to the center.

FLOWER PETAL

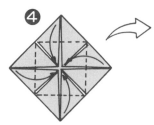

❸

Fold the corners to the center.

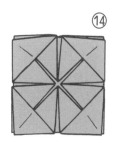

❹

Fold the corners to the center.

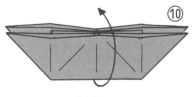

⑩

Fold over.

⑭

⑪

Open the triangles and flatten.

⑫

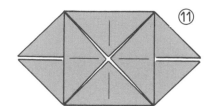

⑬

Fold over the corners.

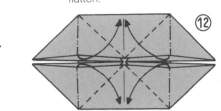

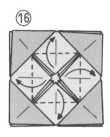

⑯

Turn over the topmost triangles.

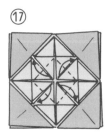

⑰

Turn over the underneath triangles.

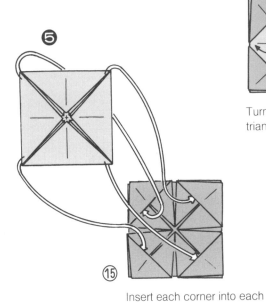

❺

⑮

Insert each corner into each pocket.

Completed.

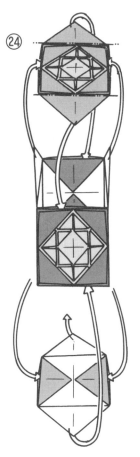

㉔

Join the top and the bottom in the same way.

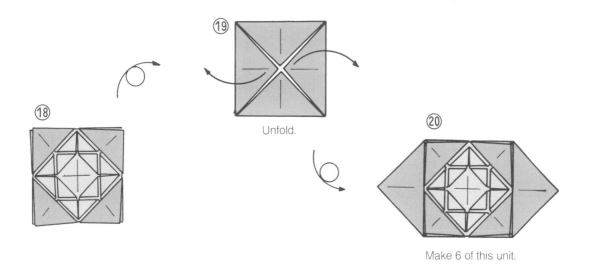

⑲ Unfold.

⑱

⑳ Make 6 of this unit.

Insert the triangle into the pocket.

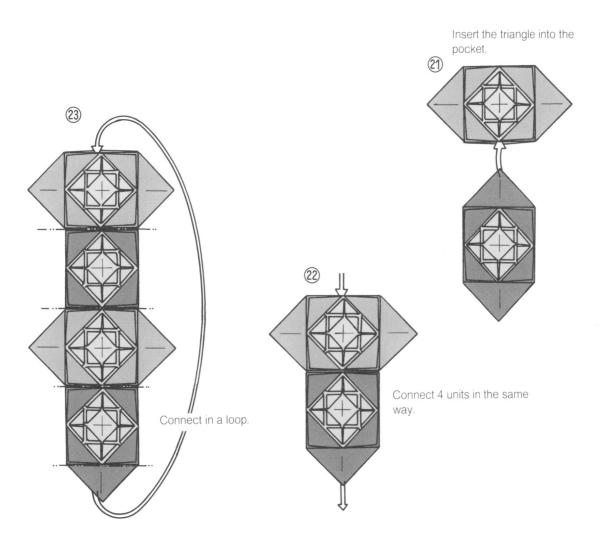

㉑

㉓

㉒ Connect 4 units in the same way.

Connect in a loop.

ELEGANCE

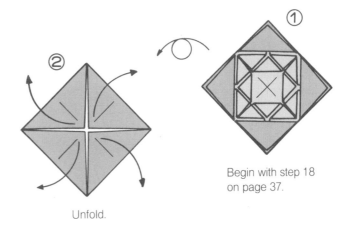

① Begin with step 18 on page 37.

② Unfold.

③
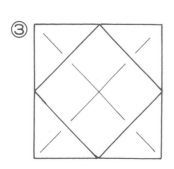

④
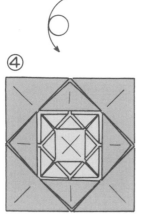

Make 6 of this unit.

⑤
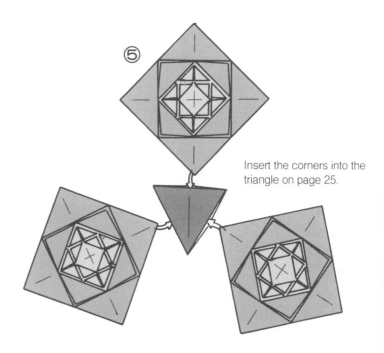

Insert the corners into the triangle on page 25.

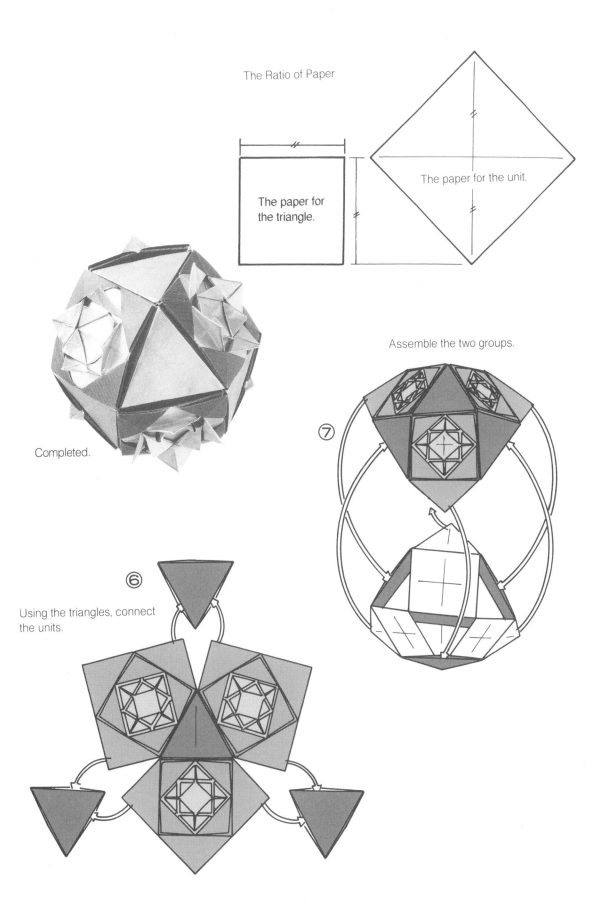

The Ratio of Paper

The paper for
the triangle.

The paper for the unit.

Completed.

Assemble the two groups.

⑦

⑥

Using the triangles, connect
the units.

DIAMOND

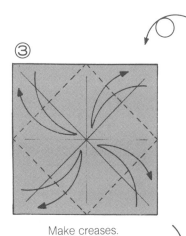

① Make creases.

② Make creases.

③ Make creases.

④

Fold to the center line.

⑤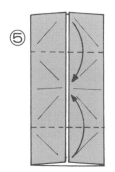

Fold to the center line.

⑥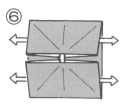

Pull out the corners.

⑦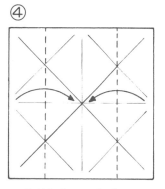

Open the triangles and flatten to form squares.

⑧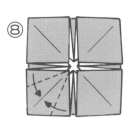

Fold to the crease.

⑨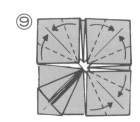

Fold the other squares in the same way.

⑯

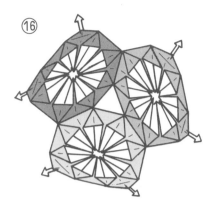

Glue the other tips together.

⑰

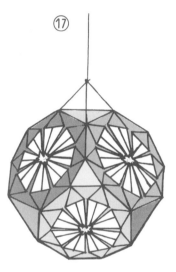

Completed.

⑮

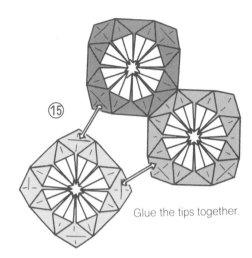

Glue the tips together.

⑭

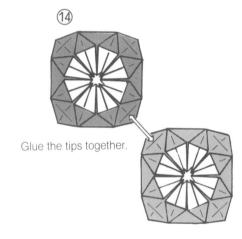

Glue the tips together.

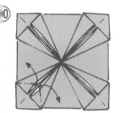

Open the triangles and flatten.

⑪

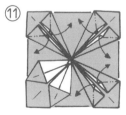

Fold the other triangles in the same way.

Fold the corners under.

⑫

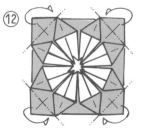

⑬ Unfold.

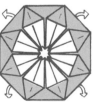

Make the same 6 units.

DICE

Begin with step 8
on page 40.

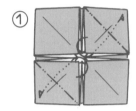

① Fold the corners in, and then
open them out again.

②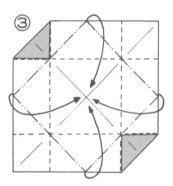

Fold the corners.

③

Fold again.

④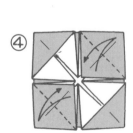

Make creases.

⑤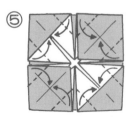

Fold all the corners.

⑥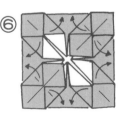

Unfold.

Connect the top and bottom
in the same way.

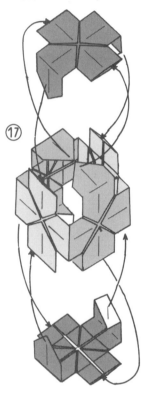

⑰

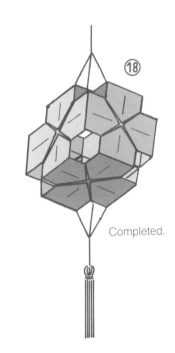

⑱

Completed.

42

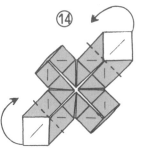

⑭ Raise the corners.

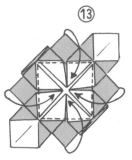

⑬ Fold the corners to the center.

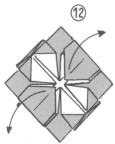

⑫ Unfold.

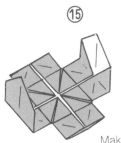

⑮ Make 6 of this unit.

⑪

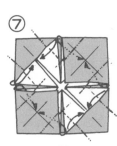

⑯ Connect 4 units by inserting the flap into each slot.

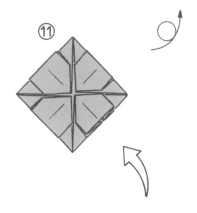

⑩ Fold the corners to the center.

Enlarged figure

⑧

⑨

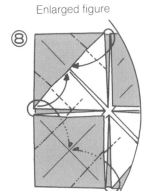

⑦ Make an inside reverse fold at each corner.

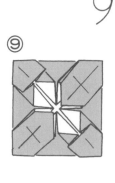

MERCURY

② ✂

✂

Cut into 4 pieces.

①

Make creases.

③

Begin with step 14
on page 43.
(Turned over)

OUTSIDE

①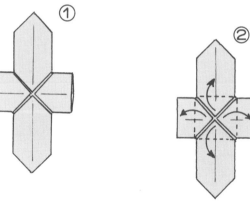

②

Fold over the triangles.

④

Make creases.

BLINTZ FOLD

⑤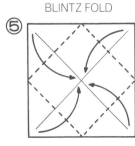

Fold the corners to the
center.

⑥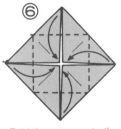

Fold the corners to the
center.

⑦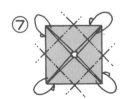

Fold the corners back.

44

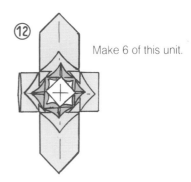

⑫ Make 6 of this unit.

See pages 42-43 for assembling.

Completed.

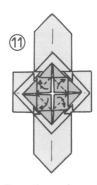

⑪

Open the underneath triangles.

⑧

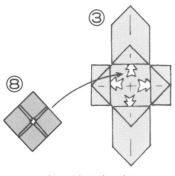

③

Insert into the slots.

⑨

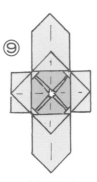

Joined unit.

⑩

Open the topmost triangles.

VENUS

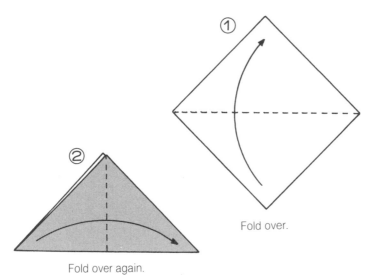

① Fold over.

② Fold over again.

③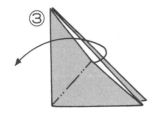

Open and flatten.

④

⑤ Turn over.

⑥ Open and flatten.

⑦ Fold to the center line.

⑧ Unfold.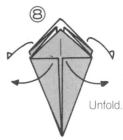

⑨ Open and flatten.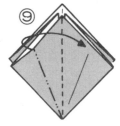

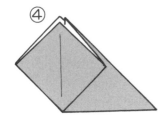
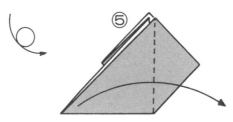
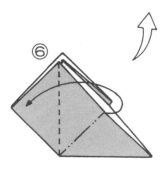

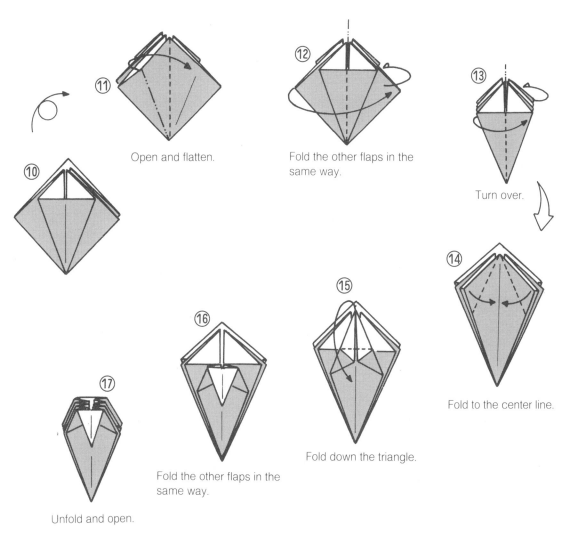

⑩

⑪ Open and flatten.

⑫ Fold the other flaps in the same way.

⑬ Turn over.

⑭ Fold to the center line.

⑮ Fold down the triangle.

⑯ Fold the other flaps in the same way.

⑰ Unfold and open.

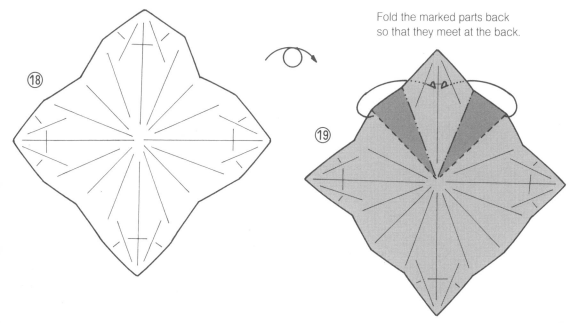

⑱

⑲ Fold the marked parts back so that they meet at the back.

Fold to the center.

⑳

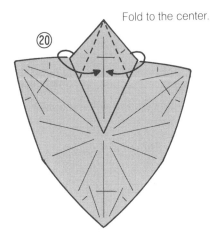

㉙

Make 40 of this unit.

Pass thread through 10 units and tie.

㉘

Seen from the side.

㉗

Fold the triangle down.

Fold on the creases as in step 20.

㉖

Open the slit a little.

㉕

Fold down the triangle.

㉑

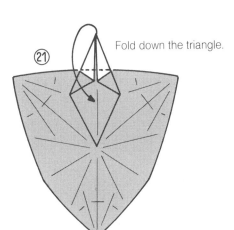

Fold the marked parts back so that they meet at the back.

㉒

Fold the marked parts back so that they meet at the back.

㉔

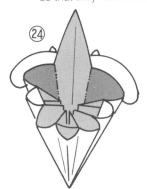

Fold to the center.

㉓

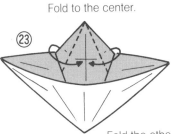

Fold the other corners in the same way.

48

㉚

See pages 11-12 for assembling the units.

Connect 10 units with thread and tie the base.

Make 4 groups of 10 units.

MAKING THE TASSEL

① Hold together a bunch of colorful strings.

② Tie the middle with a piece of string.

③ After tying, leave about 10 cm (4 inches) of string on each side of the tie.

④ Tie the two crossed strings and the bunch of string together in the middle.

Prepare two pieces of long string and tie them at the middle.

① Tie a small loop at one of the ends, to mark it.

HANGER

Prepare a loop of string for hanging.

⑤ Tie the base of the tuft.

⑥ Cut off extra string.

⑦ Trim the end.

⑧ Marking

49

PLUTO

A Variation of the design on page 46.

Begin with step 7 on page 46.

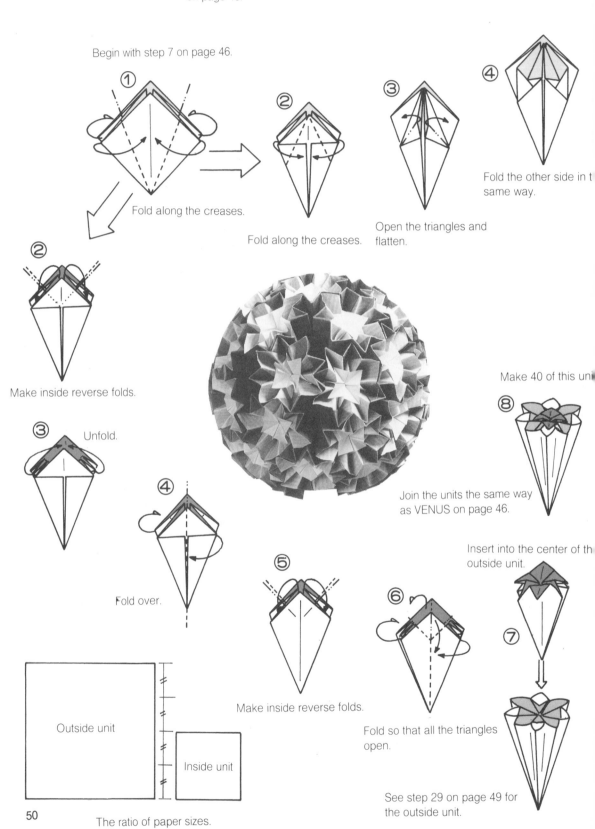

① Fold along the creases.

② Fold along the creases.

③ Open the triangles and flatten.

④ Fold the other side in the same way.

② Make inside reverse folds.

③ Unfold.

④ Fold over.

⑤ Make inside reverse folds.

⑥ Fold so that all the triangles open.

⑦

⑧ Make 40 of this unit.

Join the units the same way as VENUS on page 46.

Insert into the center of the outside unit.

See step 29 on page 49 for the outside unit.

Outside unit

Inside unit

The ratio of paper sizes.

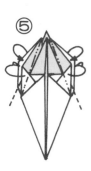

⑤

Fold each behind.

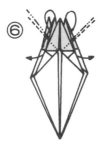

⑥

Make inside reverse folds.

Unfold.

⑦

⑧

Fold over.

Make inside reverse folds.

⑨

Fold so that the points open.

⑪

⑩

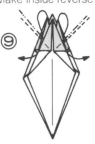

Make 40 of this unit.

⑫

Insert into
the outside unit.

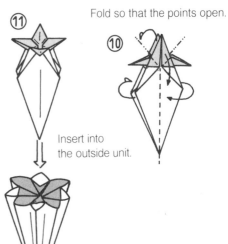

Join the units the same way
as VENUS on page 46.

See step 29 on page 48
for the outside unit.

Make 40 of the unit with
horns on page 48.

Join the units the same way
as VENUS on page 46.

①

②

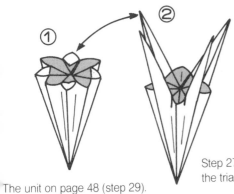

The unit on page 48 (step 29).

Step 27 on page 48 before folding
the triangles.

CROWN

Begin with step 7
on page 46.

② Unfold.

① Fold over.

③ Fold over.

④ Make creases.

⑨

↻ The same fold as step 5

⑧

⑤ Join the corners along creases.

⑥ Insert the marked part into the pocket.

⑦ Unfold.

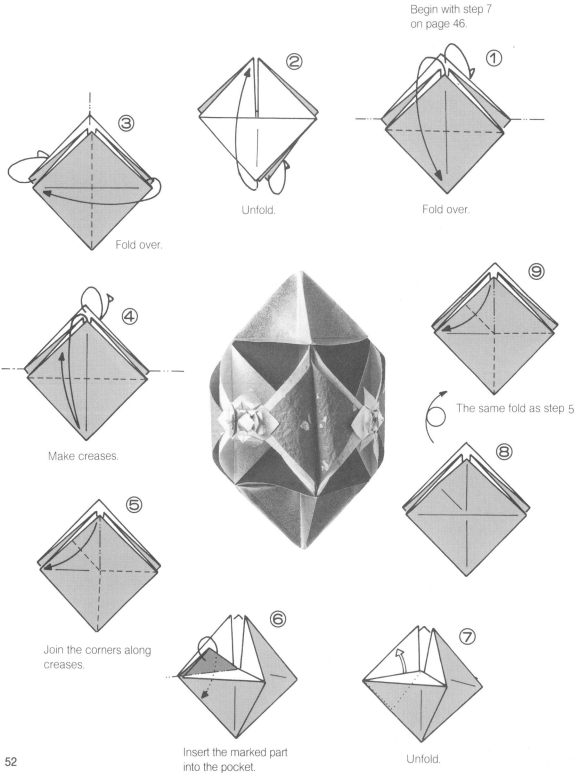

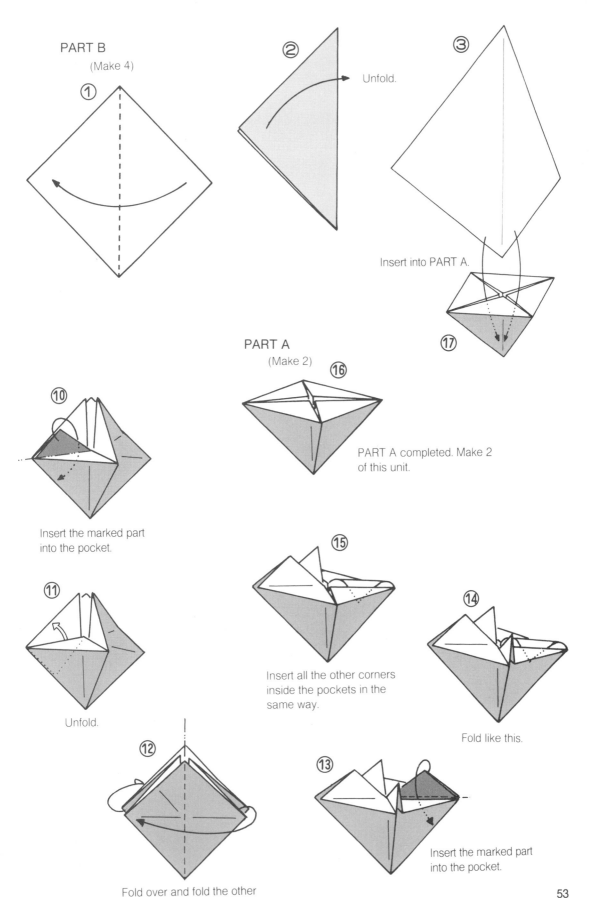

PART B

(Make 4)

① ② Unfold. ③

Insert into PART A.

⑰

PART A

(Make 2)

⑯

PART A completed. Make 2
of this unit.

⑩

Insert the marked part
into the pocket.

⑮

Insert all the other corners
inside the pockets in the
same way.

⑭

Fold like this.

⑪

Unfold.

⑬

Insert the marked part
into the pocket.

⑫

Fold over and fold the other
sides in the same way.

53

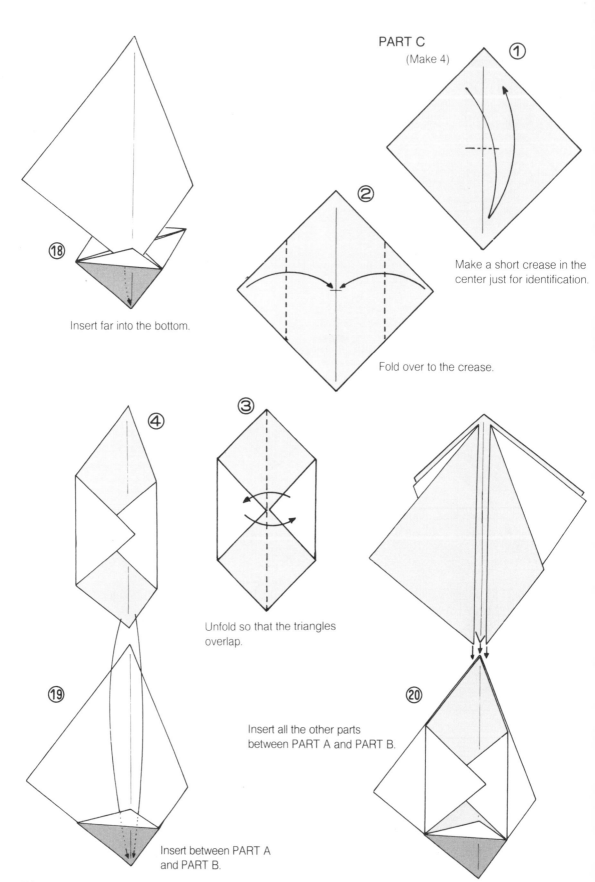

PART C
(Make 4)

① Make a short crease in the center just for identification.

② Fold over to the crease.

③ Unfold so that the triangles overlap.

④

⑱ Insert far into the bottom.

⑲ Insert between PART A and PART B.

⑳ Insert all the other parts between PART A and PART B.

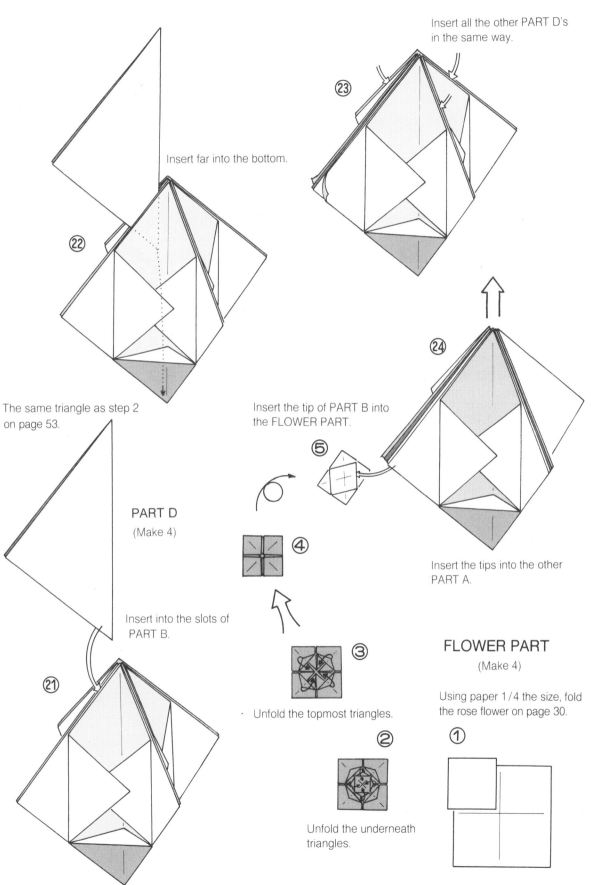

Insert all the other PART D's in the same way.

㉓

Insert far into the bottom.

㉒

The same triangle as step 2 on page 53.

PART D
(Make 4)

Insert into the slots of PART B.

㉑

Insert the tip of PART B into the FLOWER PART.

⑤

④

③

Unfold the topmost triangles.

②

Unfold the underneath triangles.

㉔

Insert the tips into the other PART A.

FLOWER PART
(Make 4)

Using paper 1/4 the size, fold the rose flower on page 30.

①

55

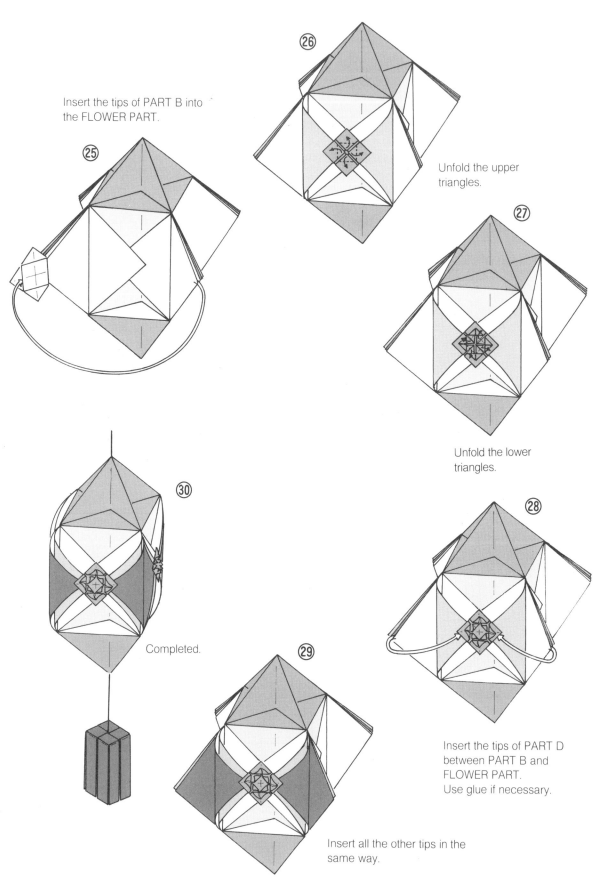

Insert the tips of PART B into the FLOWER PART.

㉕

㉖

Unfold the upper triangles.

㉗

Unfold the lower triangles.

㉘

Insert the tips of PART D between PART B and FLOWER PART.
Use glue if necessary.

㉙

Insert all the other tips in the same way.

㉚

Completed.

56

FESTIVAL 1

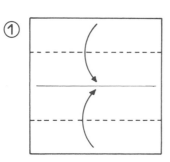

Fold along creases.

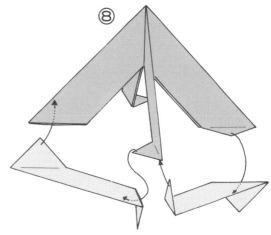

Insert and fix two units in the same way.

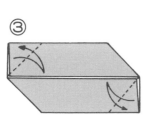

Fold the corners under.

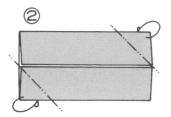

Make creases.

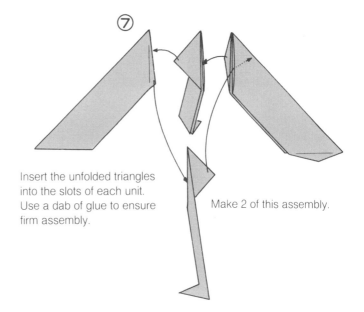

Insert the unfolded triangles into the slots of each unit. Use a dab of glue to ensure firm assembly.

Make 2 of this assembly.

Make inside reverse folds along the creases.

Make 12 of this unit.

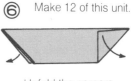

Unfold the corners.

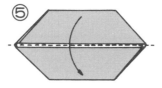

Fold over.

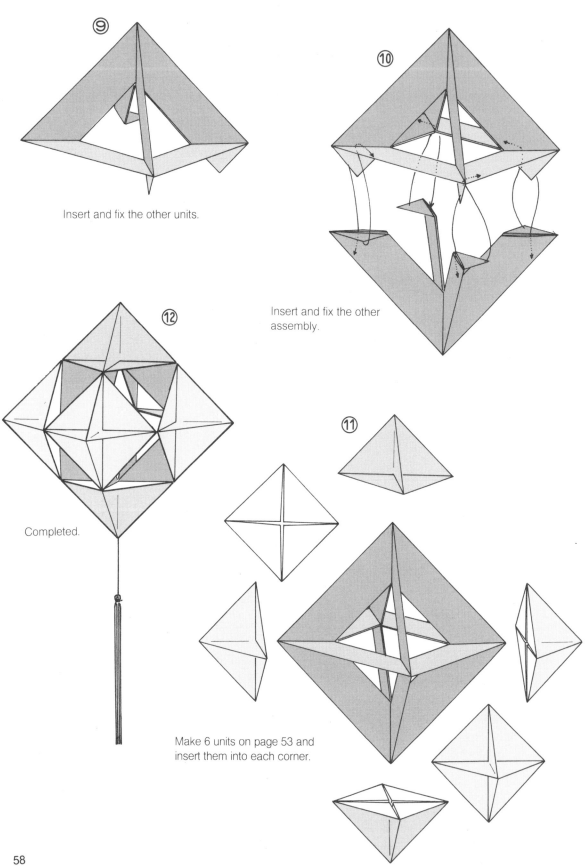

⑨ Insert and fix the other units.

⑩ Insert and fix the other assembly.

⑫ Completed.

⑪ Make 6 units on page 53 and insert them into each corner.

FESTIVAL 2

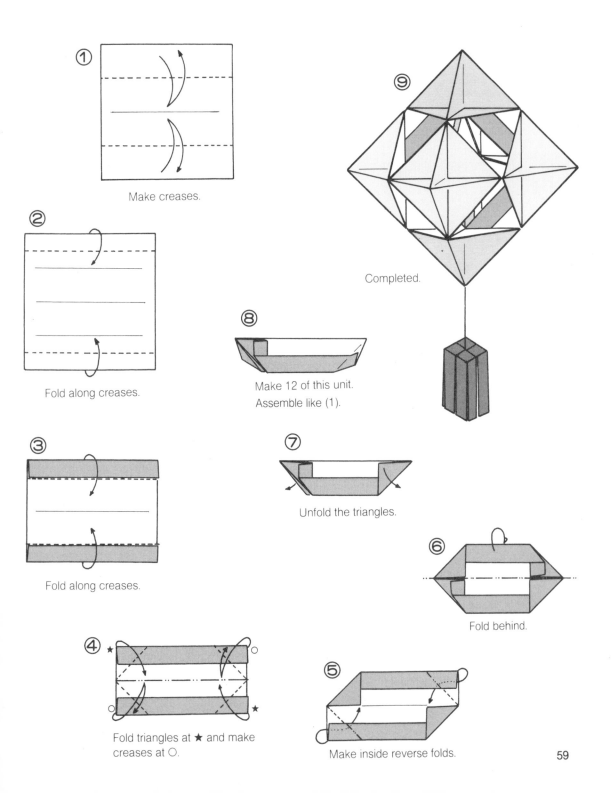

① Make creases.

② Fold along creases.

③ Fold along creases.

④ Fold triangles at ★ and make creases at ○.

⑤ Make inside reverse folds.

⑥ Fold behind.

⑦ Unfold the triangles.

⑧ Make 12 of this unit. Assemble like (1).

⑨ Completed.

RAPSODY

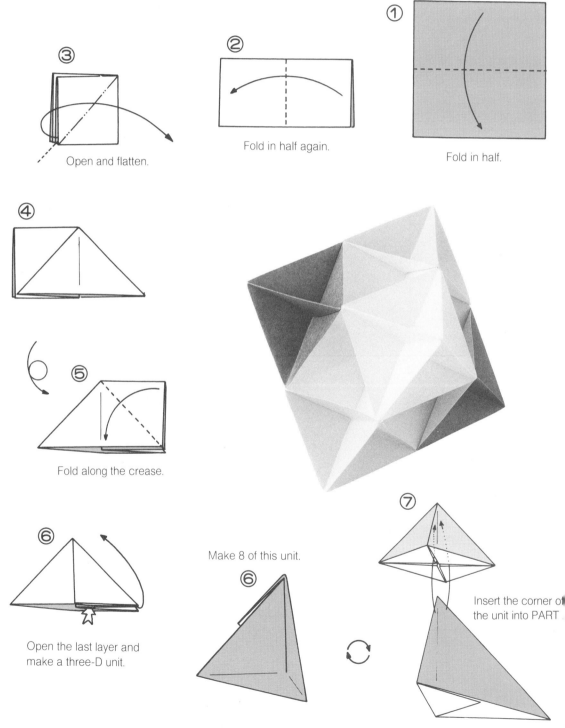

③

Open and flatten.

②

Fold in half again.

①

Fold in half.

④

⑤

Fold along the crease.

⑥

Open the last layer and
make a three-D unit.

Make 8 of this unit.

⑥

⑦

Insert the corner of
the unit into PART

60

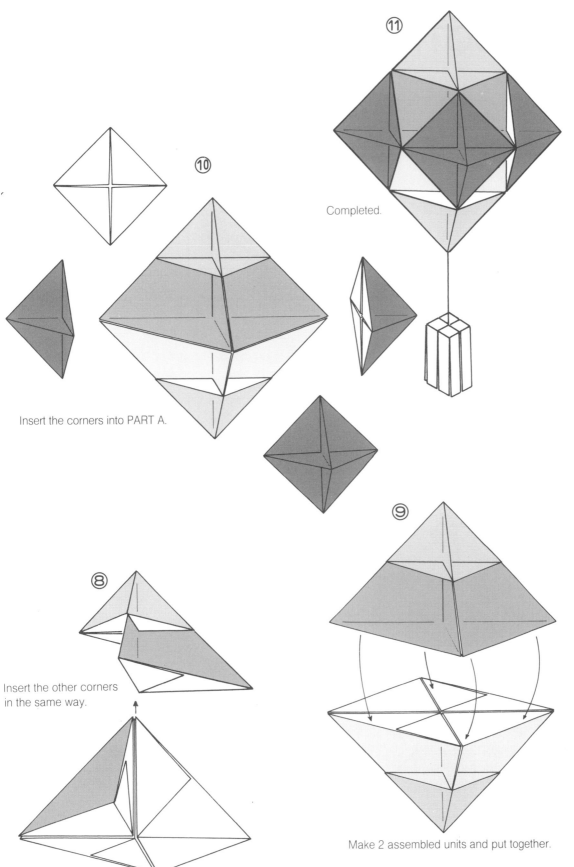

⑪

Completed.

⑩

Insert the corners into PART A.

⑨

Make 2 assembled units and put together.

⑧

Insert the other corners
in the same way.

SHOOTING STAR

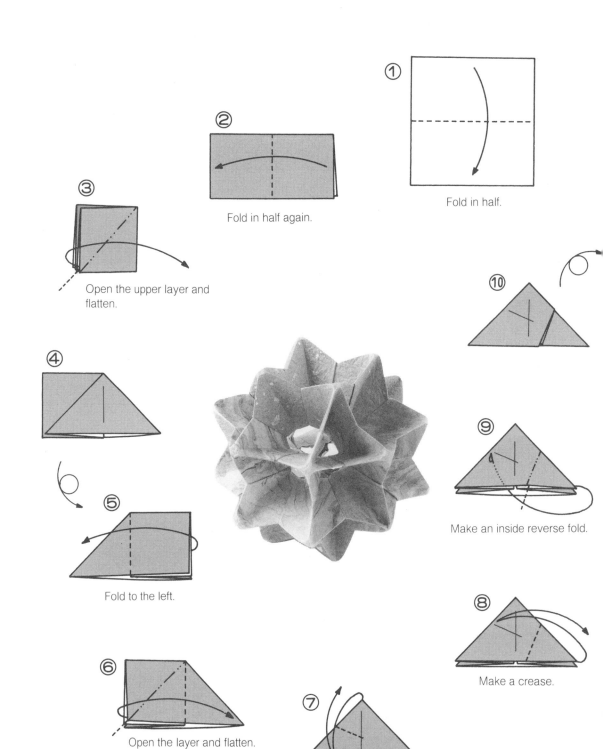

① Fold in half.

② Fold in half again.

③ Open the upper layer and flatten.

④

⑤ Fold to the left.

⑥ Open the layer and flatten.

⑦ Make a crease.

⑧ Make a crease.

⑨ Make an inside reverse fold.

⑩

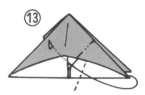

⑬ Make an inside reverse fold.

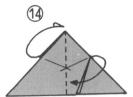

⑭ Lift the flaps.

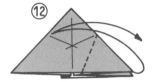

⑫ Make a crease.

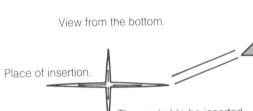

View from the bottom.

Place of insertion.

The pocket to be inserted.

⑮ Make 24 of this unit.

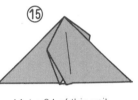

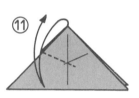

⑪ Make a crease.

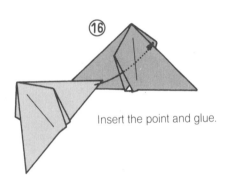

⑯ Insert the point and glue.

⑰ Insert like this.

Make 6 of these 4-unit groups.

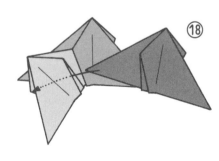

⑱

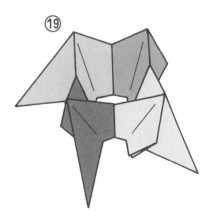

⑲

63

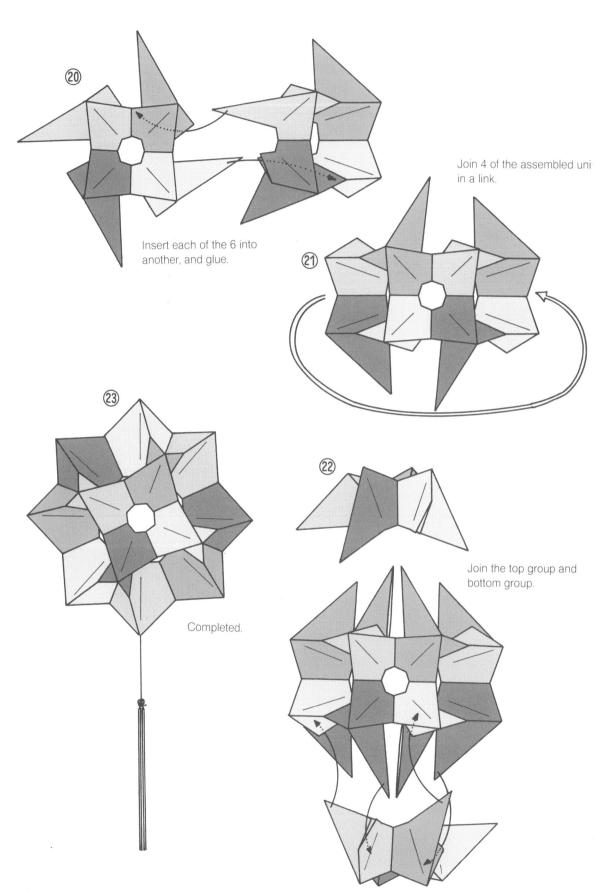

⑳

Insert each of the 6 into
another, and glue.

Join 4 of the assembled uni[t]
in a link.

㉑

㉓

Completed.

㉒

Join the top group and
bottom group.

STARFLOWER

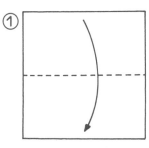

① Fold in half.

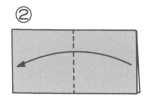

② Fold in half again.

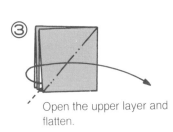

③ Open the upper layer and flatten.

④

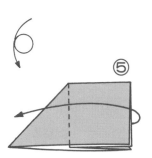

⑤ Fold to the left.

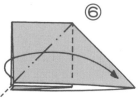

⑥ Open the layer and flatten.

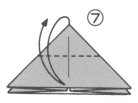

⑦ Make a crease.

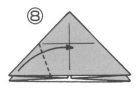

⑧ Fold along the crease.

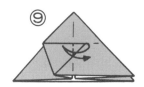

⑨ Make a crease on the center line.

⑩ Unfold.

Fold the other corners in the same way.

Push in.

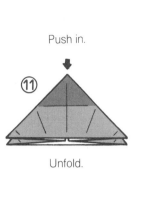

⑪

Unfold.

⑫

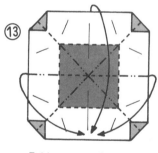

Fold the corners along the creases.

⑬

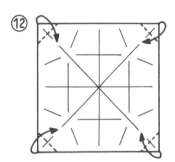

Fold up according to the creases.

⑭

Fold like this.

TYPE B

⑮

Lift the corners.

TYPE A

⑯

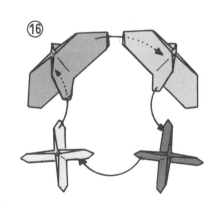

Join 4 units with care.

⑯

Insert into the pocket.

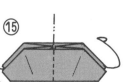

㉓

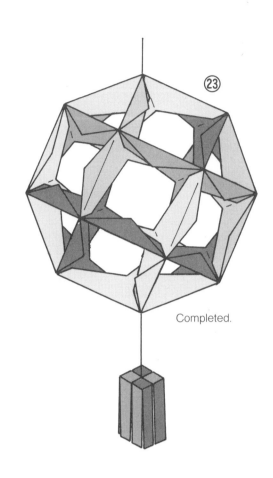

Completed.

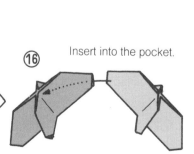

TYPE B

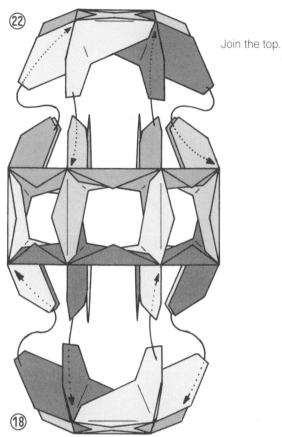

Join the top.

Fold the triangles down.

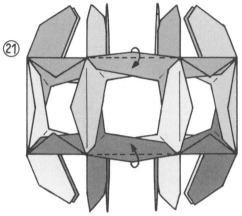

Make a link by joining 4 groups of PART A.

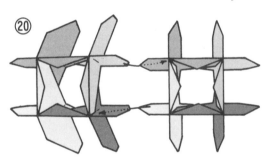

Join 2 PART A's.

Join the bottom in the same way.

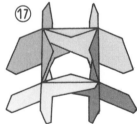

Make 2 of this assembled group.

PART A

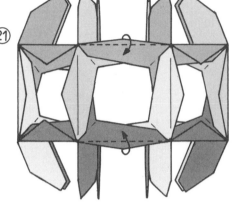

Make 4 of this assembled group.

PART B

Fold the triangle down.

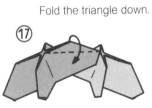

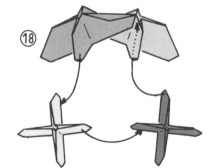

Join 4 units with care.

MORNING DEW

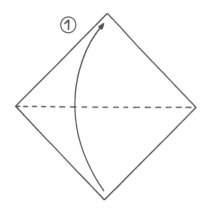

① Fold into shape of a triangle.

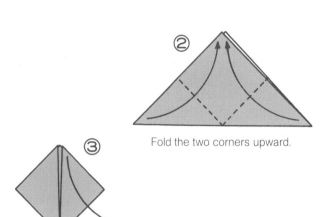

② Fold the two corners upward.

③ Unfold.

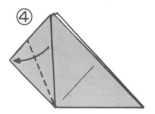

④ Fold to the right.

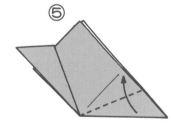

⑤ Fold up to the line.

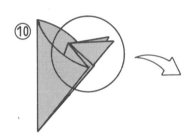

⑩

⑨ Unfold.

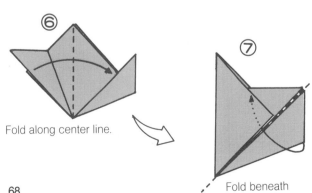

⑥ Fold along center line.

⑦ Fold beneath the upper layer.

⑧ Bring down the two flaps.

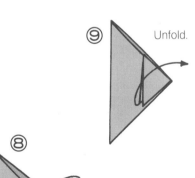

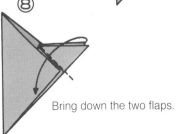

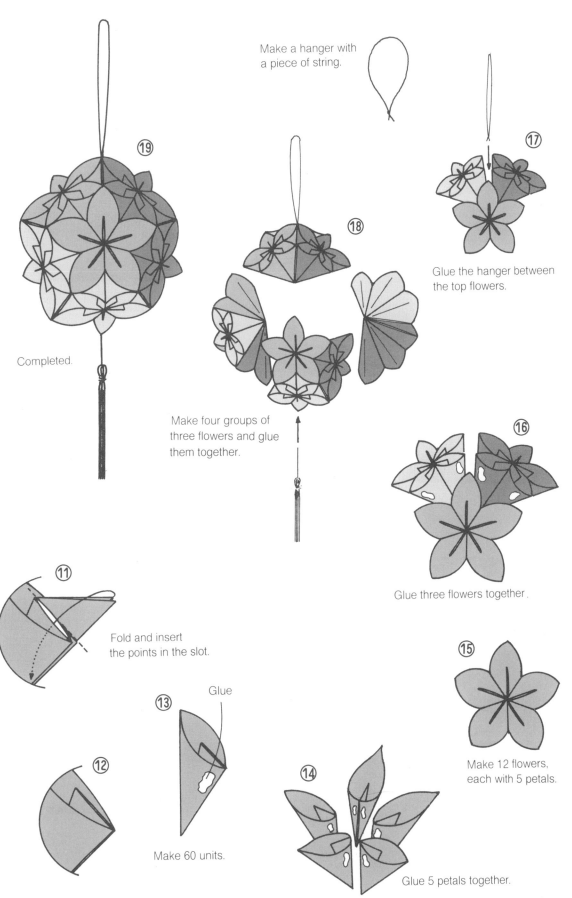

Make a hanger with a piece of string.

⑲

Completed.

⑱

Make four groups of three flowers and glue them together.

⑰

Glue the hanger between the top flowers.

⑯

Glue three flowers together.

⑪

Fold and insert the points in the slot.

⑬

Glue

⑫

Make 60 units.

⑭

Glue 5 petals together.

⑮

Make 12 flowers, each with 5 petals.

BUTTERFLY

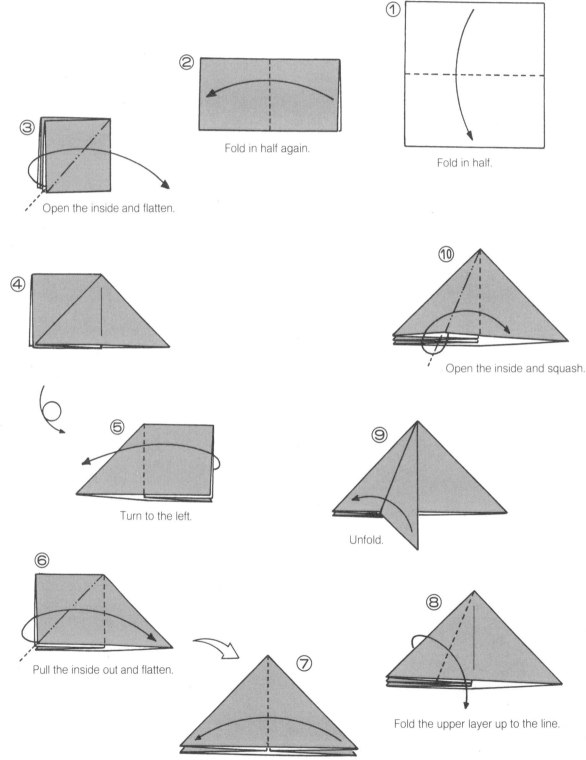

Fold in half.

Fold in half again.

Open the inside and flatten.

Turn to the left.

Pull the inside out and flatten.

Fold to the left.

Fold the upper layer up to the line.

Unfold.

Open the inside and squash.

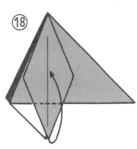

Fold the point upward.

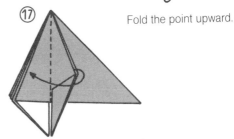

Fold only the upper layer to the left.

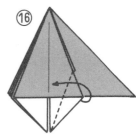

Fold up to the line.

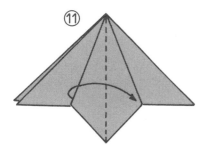

Fold to the right.

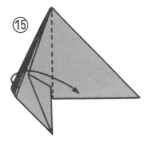

Fold only two layers to the right.

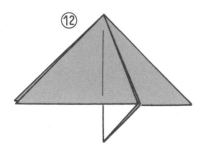

Fold the other two flaps in the same way.

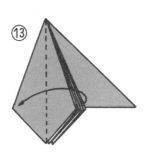

Fold all to the left.

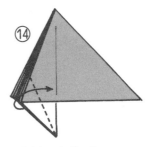

Fold up to the line.

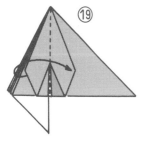
⑲

Fold the other points in the same way.

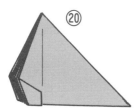
⑳

Open to the original sheet.

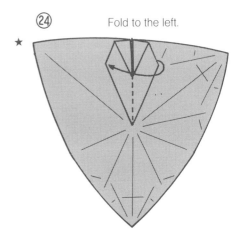
⑭ Fold to the left.

★

Fold the peak downward.

⑳

★

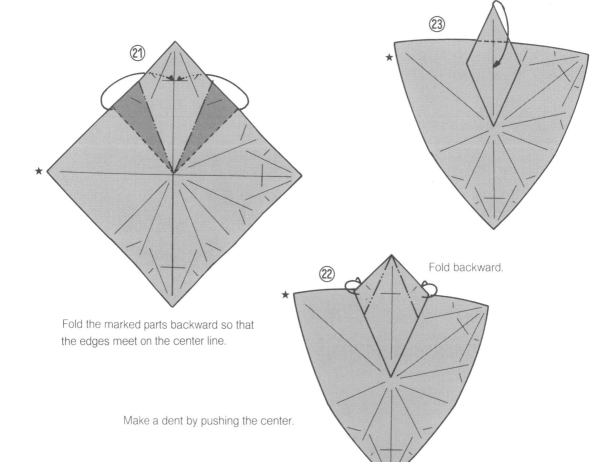

㉑

★

Fold the marked parts backward so that
the edges meet on the center line.

Make a dent by pushing the center.

㉒
★

Fold backward.

㉓
★

Fold the other corners except the
corner marked ★ in the same way.

㉕

★

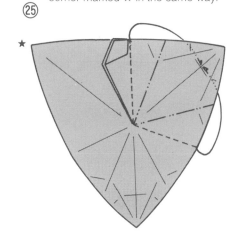

㉚

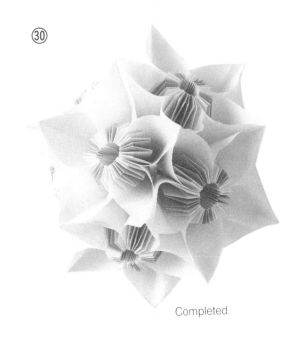

Completed.

Petals completed.

㉖

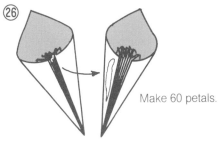

Make 60 petals.

Use a bit of glue to join them.

Five flowers glued.

㉙

㉗

Five petals are glued to make a flower.

Make 12 flowers.

Three flowers glued.

㉘

PANSY

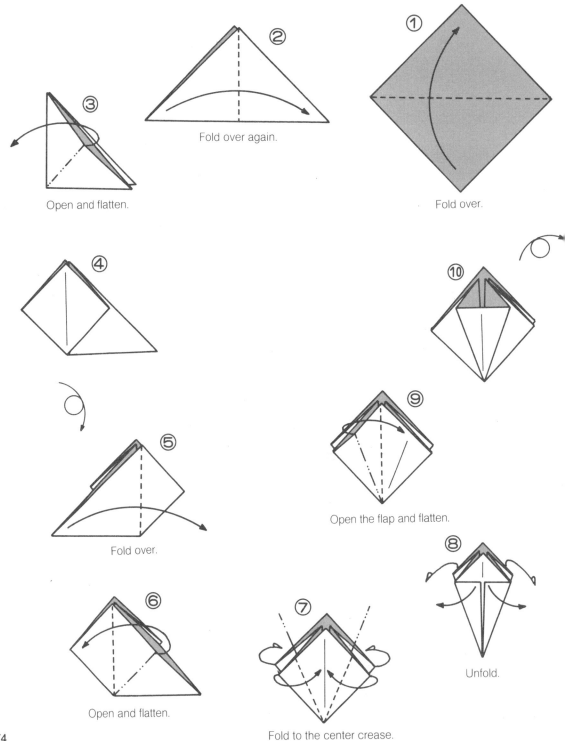

② Fold over again.

③ Open and flatten.

① Fold over.

④

⑤ Fold over.

⑥ Open and flatten.

⑦ Fold to the center crease.

⑧ Unfold.

⑨ Open the flap and flatten.

⑩

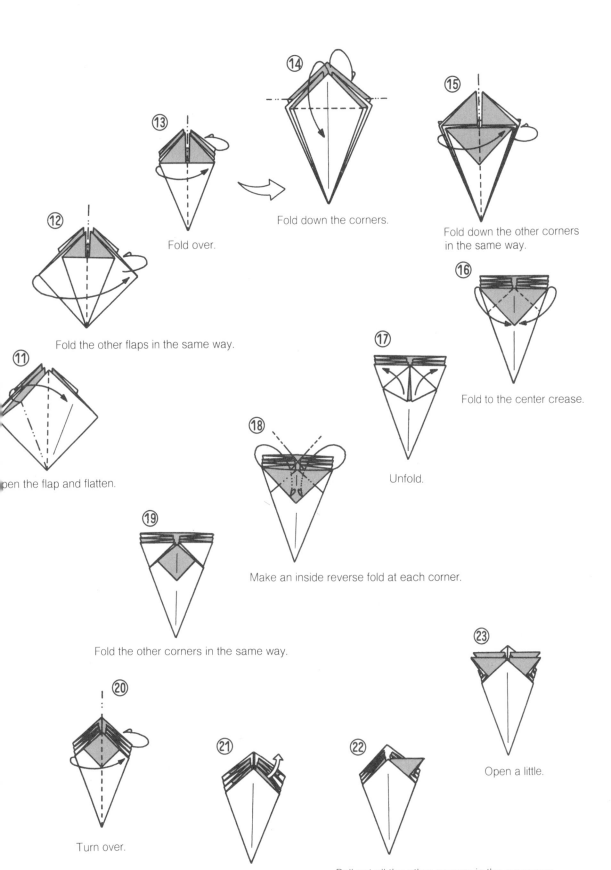

⑬
Fold over.

⑭
Fold down the corners.

⑮
Fold down the other corners
in the same way.

⑫
Fold the other flaps in the same way.

⑯

⑰
Fold to the center crease.

⑪
Open the flap and flatten.

⑱
Unfold.

⑲
Fold the other corners in the same way.

Make an inside reverse fold at each corner.

⑳
Turn over.

㉑
Pull out the corner.

㉒
Pull out all the other corners in the same way.

㉓
Open a little.

75

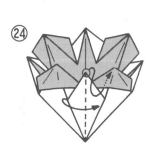

㉔

Insert the tip ○ under the pocket.

㉕

Insert the other tips in the same way.

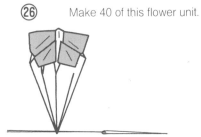

㉖ Make 40 of this flower unit.

Pass a thread through all 10 units.

Join the units the same way
as VENUS on page 46.

VARIATION

Begin with step 15 on page 75.

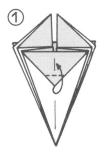

①

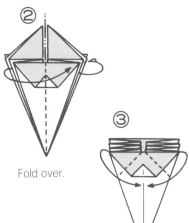

②

Fold over.

③

The other steps are the same as those from 16 .